BRUISE
SONGS

BRUISE
SONGS

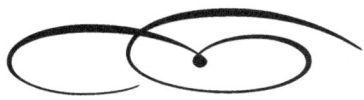

Steve Davenport

STEPHEN F. AUSTIN STATE UNIVERSITY PRESS

Stephen F. Austin State University Press
P.O. Box 13007, SFA Station
Nacogdoches, TX 75962
sfapress@sfasu.edu
www.sfasu.edu/sfapress
936-468-1078

ISBN: 978-1-62288-302-8
First Edition
Printed in the United States

Cover Design: Quint Charvis
Original Photo: Joe Johnston
Editorial Staff: Jerri Bourrous and Jakayla Murphy

*for Sophie, Tess, Hannah, and Nora
and Celia, who paved the way*

Contents

And terrible fishes to seize my flesh,
Such as a living man might fear

— Edna St. Vincent Millay, "Burial"

Yes. The music will do that—take pain and pour it
someplace else for a while.

— Tyehimba Jess,
"Sam Patterson, Harlem, NY: Dec. 12, 1924"

Dear Horse I Rode In On

— for Garin Cycholl

Mine is the curl of rind
the lick of salt the shaved
barkings of all these lines
or limes I cut and squeeze
for bruise songs, my cowboy
brag. Rhyme is everything
in song. You done me wrong.

Terrible Fishes

— for Susan Yount

> "An occasional, brief break from the water while
> trying to spit out a hook is fine; a quick splash
> while lunging for a bug on the surface? Okay.
> But spontaneously leaping ten feet in the air and
> soaring a few feet horizontally? Unacceptable.
> Horrifying."
> — Ted Gregory, *Mary Jane's Ghost*

The Illinois River's raining Silver
Carp near Peoria, long thunder
fields of bouncing pit bull carp,
reverse whack-a-mole of M-80 carp,
catapulting, trampolining carp, crack
-splashing, glass-slamming carp, boat
-jumping, break-your-jaw carp, electric
seizures of carp, clouds of species-
devouring carp, crazy grid of under
water mines triggered blown upward
in terrible sprays of carp, of falling carp
reassembling in multiples of insisting carp.

This river's no ankle dream, no prom
night Boone's Farm folk song, no blue
gill nibbling at your toes, no cherrybomb
anticipation or nervous zippers or buttons
or fingers for virgins in cars parked
on asphalt abutting muddy banks.

This is fish porn, not The Golden Carp
of Forgiveness and Clear Waters.
This is scrape your washboard in awful song.
This is bang your big drum in be-gone song.
This is my two-chord, carp-killin' river song.
Sing it with me down by the water.

99 Bottles of Beer and 27 Chickens

At the beginning of the world,
a Sunday, I jumped
from a moving car,
reached high
into a tree for a bird,
and took its wings
because I needed them.
Which comes first,
chicken or egg?
Unless you're hungry,
who cares?

At the beginning of the world,
a Sunday, I swallowed
those wings and flapped
down I-72 to Decatur,
where I measured words
twice, cut once, made good
my third chance.
Which comes first,
word or thought?
If you're hungry,
who cares?

At the beginning of the world,
a Sunday, Decatur, Illinois,
in my second-floor nest,
700 West Main Street,
I drank 99 bottles of beer,
ate 27 chickens,
and made pipe bombs
of poems I calibrated
in 14s and 12s.
My fingers shined
like greasy bones.

At the beginning of the world,
a Sunday, it was April.
I didn't know April
was Poetry Month.
I didn't know I was
writing yodel sonnets,
and I don't know
which comes first,
song or poetry.
I know I was hungry.
I know the world began.

Dear wings, Dear I-72,
at the beginning of the world.
Dear West Main, Dear Decatur,
at the beginning of the world.
Dear Lynn,
at the beginning of the world

all those Poetry Months ago.
I know three things.
History is sticky.
Chicken and beer are good.
This is a love poem.

Afflatus Behind Dumpsters in America
— for upfromsumdirt

I'd say Hello, Friday,
you sexy wolf,
roller of big cigars,
full belly dragging
through Cuban waters
and green hostilities,
maker of the first beginning,
which is light and breath
blowing big ships
and new routes,
you river of mash rolling,
you 100 bottles
of beer on the wall,
I'd take you down,
Friday, and pass
you around, and you
might be the emperor
of ice cream
they talk about,
muscular accountant
of concupiscence,
keeper of the ledger
I don't want read
while I'm living,
while I have children
who like ice cream
more than bodies,

and there were bodies
being bodies
and I hope I'm right
about the ice cream.

I'd say hello, Friday,
and we'd rip
the long flesh
together, string
couplets of sinew
and blood round
all the available bellies,
we'd go thigh
to high valley
in praise song
to deep hallelujah,
moist hallelujah,
we would,
but don't tell
my children, Friday,
my daughters,
don't tell them
I'm here,
these days,
behind this dumpster,
around the corner,
waiting for change,
an improvement
of my circumstances,
and I'm not the only one,

back to the wall,
criss-cross applesauce
in America,
because, Friday,
these days, you're ass
to patchy grass,
no better than Thursday,
Tuesday's thick twin,
kissing cousin
to Monday and Wednesday,
who blame each other
for everything.

I'd say Hello, Friday,
or America,
what's the difference,
and forgive you
this dumpster,
but truth's important too,
which doesn't mean
this isn't a poem,
which doesn't mean
it is either,
which doesn't mean
it isn't also a treatise,
a dissertation
on afflatus,
sudden gathering,
wind-blown kick start,
a disquisition

on divine breath,
see Holy Spirit
for English majors,
see original invention,
see afflatus@wikipedia.org,
or maybe it's a spell,
all pork pie hat
and Godot tattoo
and iambic inspiration,
or a dream, America,
I need a dream
about a Friday
that switches things up
by tomorrow, Saturday,
which is a math problem
if you think Sunday's
a map of soft deserts
and leafy mountaintops.
See life behind dumpster.

Here's the thing,
O Grain of Sand,
O Wild Flower,
I never once saw
the world
in either of you,
or heaven, though I had
good teachers.
O Winds of Change,
what change?

Wild Flower's
got nothing
on the five kinds
of stank trapped here
behind this dumpster
by city planners.
See afflatus.
See dead air.
But I'll make do, Friday,
and truth is
it's dinner time
and this half a chicken
wing ain't bad as it looks.

So Friday, this here's
my disquisitional poem
about poetry or afflatus
or dumpster life, here,
around the corner.
Some days I write
in the dead air
to freak a dead end,
a long wait for meaning,
like I learned
from good teachers,
but these days,
America, Friday,
I'm studying accessibility.
I'm blowing this breath,
good or bad, your way.

In the Dream of Rhyming Nicki Minaj

In the dream
of rhyming
Nicki Minaj
with decoupage
I watch part time
library workers
stuff opaque tubes
with retired souvenirs
three glass cases
worth of fingers
knuckles toes
cut clipped
swapped like coins
or bottle caps
in 1899 or 1949
and seal them
like messages
in bottles
or labeled boxes
in warehouses
for the next
lynching exhibit
and I'm supposed to
make all that rhyme
for my thesis committee

In the dream
of rhyming

Nicki Minaj
with Billy Jack
I open Facebook
to photo photo photo
from the north
of Iceland
Godafoss Myvatn Hverir
healing waters
and mud baths
and waterfalls
and one person
floating on
The Dictionary
of Mind Rhymes
I'm supposed to
use to explain
immigration patterns
and the invention
of race in verse
to my students
tomorrow

In the dream
of rhyming
Nicki Minaj
with Wizard of Oz
I'm riding shotgun
with my 15-yr-old
driver's permit
daughter Hannah

from Urbana who's
aux cord blasting
whiplash blink fast
and I'm taking notes
Minaj 101
wishing Hannah
a poet's brains
a poet's fangs
her body
her body
and what she
makes rhyme
with monster
as she drives

At the Moment of Conception a Train and a Bird

— written with Lillian-Yvonne Bertram

My body the long oath browning the red pages of his ledger
red as the town's young glass is red. The brown beginnings
of our math grinding bone on bone, the snakemouthed
night closes in with its small winds, its blue bottles of every
size, and its songs, bird song, train song, each divisible by
the other.

Dear Aphasia

Man sits in a room.
You're the saddle
on my parakeet,
the tangled soup
on my alphabet feet.
Man walks into
a bar. Man walks into
an ER. Man walks into
a cave and forgets
the names of his
daughters. Bartender
says if there's a
hole that ain't
a bucket.

I'm losing my place.
Saddle. Syllable.
I say Humpty Dumpty
without words.
Hickory Dickory
Doc says your
husband's in
the middle of a stroke.
You're the tangle,
the lock twitching
in my tumbled sheet.

Dickory Doc asks
can you feel
your pieces?

Man walks into
an ER with a bucket.
Man walks into
a bar with a bucket.
The buckets share a hole.
Bartender asks what
rhymes with bucket?
Say it if you can.
Bartender says
there once was
a bucket in
a cave in ?
I look at him.
Nantucket, Doc

says. There once was
a man
from Nantucket
who lived in
a hole in a bucket.
Do you understand?
Dear Aphasia,
you're the cotton in
concrete, the lost
syllable in
repeat. There's a

hole and there's a
bucket and there's a
man in a room.

Dear Cerebral Angiogram

I love you, Rainbow.

I send mountaintop and strum. I send three chords and a femoral artery. I send My Sasquatch bearing Inks of Plenty.

I drop flowers before your long way of looking at me, of making train stretch for syllables.

I lift this ode to your Northern compass, your colors, your branching out, your streaks and steadies, your way of rounding into view, the way you Missouri my Mississippi, muddy the bend, flood my plain way of being with dye to light me up.

I send carotid artery and a list of problems. Fistula. Anomaly. I ask that you open lines of dialogue.

I find the clot you leave under the bruise. I ask that you open lines of time.

I bend a knee to your reach, your perfect nose.

Flower Pot, I love your crazy hair.

This Living in the Weeks After
— for Okla Elliott (1987-2017)

This living in the weeks
after, a waiting for lines
to move, shadings
so light sometimes
they don't take
and notes repeat.

This waiting, a smelting
of selves, leavings of slag
and gases and pig iron,
ink returning to pens.

This living, when it works,
a shaping, a stacking,
a warehousing
of patterns, a book
for making the long blur,
the waiting, particulate.

I Marry My Stroke

I saw you at the liquor store yesterday not one hour after we rubbed fenders in the library parking lot and fussed all the way into Periodicals, where we made out like sticky magazines. You get around.

I admit my heart is wormy and I am downwardly mobile. Admit your sails are made of cheesecloth and your relationships end where they start. Let's fight.

I'll be your swizzle stick if you'll be my flight of three martinis. 1: Insert Another Quarter. 2: We Are Nearing The End. 3: Doornail, Dead As.

I had a lover once who milked the last bit of me into a casing no thicker than a glance and fired it at me as I got out of bed to find my phone.

I lost words for exit and re-enter. I have a hole in my bucket. I should keep my enemies close.

I hate you. Faithfulness is overrated. Marry me.

Dear Happy Ending

It rained last week
for a hundred years
and change,
bitter change
like ninety-nine nuts
for one squirrel
and one nut
for ninety-nine,
loose change
like the weight
of bodies depends
on the neighborhoods
they come from,
the ones they fall in.
Neighborhood
may not be
the right word.

Happy Ending,
forgive me.
How much longer?
Are we there yet?
I have to pee
and I want
the ninety-nine
everyone wants.

Last Thursday
during Happy Hour,
over cocktail wieners,
pitchers of beer,
and buckets
of popcorn,
thunder rattled
like ammo bins
three nights straight
and it was good
because it kept
everyone inside
while the place
burned and we got
what we deserved,
being mostly water
and self-interested.

Dear Happy Ending,
your friend list looks
like a family reunion.
You should get out
more, meet people,
improve the stock,
give us all a chance.

When I was fifteen,
astronauts stepped
down onto the moon,
dividing it forever

with a flag
and some God.
They tracked moon
dust back into the cabin.
It smelled, they said,
like gunpowder.
Of course, it did,
and mankind
didn't mean mankind.
That was the day
I grew shark fins,
a couple of whiskers,
and a hard line
of self-interrogation.

Dear Happy Ending,
there's a reason
why empires collapse
and folks who restrict
membership with gates
and property guns
get eaten by fire ants.
I too want to live
in a tall, round house
with no windows,
no moat, no drawbridge.
On the roof
a water park with lights

and a helicopter.
It's not a lot
to ask.

For art I was once
half bird, half dynamo,
a flapping, feathery
whir of parts
that stole the sun
and divided it
into many things,
into water and glint,
into chaff and spark,
into salt and peter,
into bang and whoosh.
We are far
from those days,
the sun's old way
of doing business,
and I can't remember
where some things
are buried.

Dear Happy Ending,
twenty days after
the moon turned
to gunpowder,
Manson's gang
went helter skelter
on some gated folks.

That was wrong
in a different way,
so they went to prison.
Parole is harder now
for some folks
because there's no
forgiveness.
The victims' families
make sure of that
with their bill of rights.
I want a new bill
of rights
and flying lessons.
I want to kill
bad guys
one by one
and go home
in my helicopter
to my fountain
of lights,
my ninety-nine
nuts.

Next month,
it will rain
for decades.
The past tense
of shit will be shot.
We should all be shot.
I shit you not.

I shoot you twice
because the world,
Happy Ending,
is a hard place
for most of us.
I think you know that.
I think you planned it
that way.

Broken Chord

— written with Lillian-Yvonne Bertram

You are the woman
from the television show who would rather
be sedated than cry—my one friend
always this species of correct
analysis and application, all eye
and murder where blues concern.
Yesterday went wrong and tomorrow's
a scene you won't want to live to. Like the queer
girls who bite the bitter stream of marriage
and manage, we sharpen our thirteen ways,
blackbirds scattering back into focus, before
we leap into what little moonlight
can romance—*He said he God*—
and fall, butcher scraps for tubs,
offal for new skewers.

Repeat, Monster, Repeat

— for Lillian-Yvonne Bertram

1.

Barbell's a palindrome for eyeballing
balance and the rising weight of distance
in matters that flap off shoulders like birds,
tumble down stairs like body parts in boxes.
Barbell's a palindrome for the way want
is split by need cranked tight for clean and jerk.
Barbell's a palindrome of fists squeezing.

2.

Want's the latest shot wad and who doesn't
love a pair of boots with metal studs screwed
into her soles and she's learning long guns
in her repeating window thirty feet
from a field dressed with another's winter
kill. Next boy's a barbell for verbing God.
She makes a note to write that down. Clean, jerk.

3.

Sky's a long bruise of bodies splayed, properties
of ink and familiar reach, patterns scanned
like voice prints pushing same old river weight,
note to note, in one ear and out, over falls
far from any economy of road,
and here, one woman, you, mass pulling mass
or massacre. Repeat, monster, repeat.

In the Dead Air

Night tongues the low slur
like an oar turning swamp
peat and vines until the sun,
rising,

breaks through the blinds,
the ceiling a mural of cracks,
chipped paint, and a fan that,
wobbling,

garbles the slamp of body
on body in sheets and liturgies
past the mind, memories below
thinking.

Something more a body
wants in the dead light
of more breathing, all this
waiting,

than grind to clutch of muscle
and back to clock radio,
but what? Room shrunk,
done?

I Divorce My Stroke

Frabjous morning, Punch.

Your Judy says Hello Wavy Pattern, Crazy Map. Hello Motel
Wallpaper, Heavy Drapes, Pizza Box, Ashtray, Bed. Hello to
this postcard. Hey, Stamp. Hi, Wet Spot.

Together we salute you. Hello Bastard. Your Wallop of
Yore? Bloat. What rhymes with peek-a-boo.

Callooh from Judy. Callay's mine.

Elegy for Another Friend Who's Not
Yet Dead Sonnet

Mixed in a gas station oil drum and poured in forms
at construction sites liquored with motorcycle
angels and union cards, that friend. Born a clear lake
to grow a long river, raised a bay to become
the sea, he rose, yes. Making hot church at the mic
in triple time and raw word, rough song for lovers,
yes, and over a book, amen, and a bottle
of Long Knives at a table out back, he preaches.
We're standing here, all of us, not yet dead, making
fast plans and fists we think matter, drinking, waiting
for the horses with eyes out to ford the river
and load us on flat boats to pull us back across.
We're drinking here, all of us, at our friend's table.
He's smoking and writing, the horses gathering.

End of the Line

3 AM. Moonlight,
stars. How'd we
run out of road
and gas? Countries,
currency? Spaces
where our differences
mattered? We followed
that high, long river
country to country,
currency to currency,
until it dipped under
ground and left us.
We had the sun
but it went too
and took the flame
and the long bluffs
we might have used
for cover. When's
the last time

that plastic cooler
was something more
than a chair, a bag
of cheese, and two,
three cans of beer
floating in water
like insurance?
Why these words

now that doodling's
as good a use
of paper, of lead
or ink as argument
or explanation
or petition,
heavenly or not?
3 AM. Moon.
Fuck it. I'm tired

of thinking, talking
about the somethings
or nothings that bracket
this world, the transit,
its terrible beauty,
deep or flat black
to light, off to on to off,
click to blinding white,
then calm or long pain.
I'm tired of endings
that have no meaning
beyond the stories
we make up. When's
the last time you saw
a bird? I'm tired

of God. Yesterday,
an hour past dusk
we left our last village,
flipped the last switch.

From the rise, we saw
its mushroom of lights
blur out and we drove.
3 AM. Moon's a scarred
palm. Here at the end
of the line's a path
made by cows walking
tree line and fence
to grazing fields. We'd

go but where? Ain't
nothing left but
distance. We'd make
love but the clocks
are broken. We'd die
before the land
gets us, but how?
Name a way. 3 AM.
A rash of stars. We
wait, hearts catfishing,
belly to throat,

trawling for stroke.
Remember that night,
the convertible
we drove from bar
to keg to liquor store,
the land full and loud,
until we found a swing
set under a lamp post

in the upper reaches

of a city park and rutted
in the grass or gravel
because the land
was good. 3 AM. Moon's
a pisspot. Here's one.
Your plane's over water
that's run bad.

You've lost your wings.
Poison's wormed through
every exchange, spread
one part to the next.
You're falling. Sick. What

to do with time? Joke. Moon
falls in a sky and no one's.
Joke. Three warm cans

of beer and no gas. Joke.
Moon. Joke. Two people walk

into an empty bar. 3 AM.

Money Shot

Many years ago, I wrote you a fan letter. Called you Rocket Man. Liquid Tremors. Called you Publicity. I was young, a poet in search of an identity. On Shell Oil property that summer, rocking roads in 100° weather two miles from the canal, predictable American Bottom humidity and refinery stink, trucks to direct, oil sprayed and bubbling, gravel to rake over it, big roller on the way, I listened to a born-again summer worker, college boy like me, talk about Jesus.

He suggested I read the Bible. That evening, a Friday, I did. I white-knuckled it. I squeezed until Genesis did me in. All those names. One had something to do with wrestling. That night I told myself I would sign all of my poems Naphtali. I told no one else, and I quit God before we got started.

Some guys get prostate cancer and have to shoot their dicks up so they can have sex. That's the plan, and they're lucky to have it. A buddy I know told me he spent one New Year's Eve in the emergency ward with needles draining blood from his hard-on. He had a New Year's Eve party to get to. One day with a heart heavy as a sack of stag balls, I'll write a poem about it. I'll dedicate it to all those guys and their needles and pumps buried in their nuts and, to be careful, to God.

It's the new plan, Shooter. Poetry for broken systems. Insurance rider attached.

When I was five or six and dutifully peeing in the toilet instead of wetting my bed, I picked up the slip-joint pliers my father had left on the tank lid like a challenge. I lined up the jaws with the head of my little self and squeezed. The pliers clamped into place. I screamed. My father hustled in and undid the grip. I named my second dog Freud.

Some guys have strokes. Stroke doc said boo to me. Said mine was minor, said I'm lucky. Said cryptogenic. Said who knows. Naphtali struggled. That's what he stands for.

Many times you got tangled, Shooter, with my heart and led me, eager buck, to that half-basement apartment where I stood for an hour and held the baby that wasn't mine so her mother, who was someone's wife, could answer a midnight emergency call at the hospital a half-mile away. The same apartment, where a month later I had to crawl out the bathroom window, ground-level, as she stalled, fumbled the chain lock.

I don't remember the baby crying. I'm not thanking you for that.

In fact, Shooter, Money Shot, I'm not talking to you anymore. You ain't what you used to be. Which was everything. Which was. Don't get me wrong.

Night of Zeroes on the Loose

It snowed like James Brown
the year I chased thoughts
down thick tubes to China
or maybe it was the night
of happy sex machines
in grad school get up-pa
get on up get up-pa
that made me rethink
numbers

It wasn't the Stones
or Etta James rolling five-
star biscuits on the tables
of content we buttered hot
with Isaac Hayes footnotes
that long winter we studied
ones and zeroes in the deep
beds of up-pa get on up
get up-pa but it could
have been

When I say we shook
our moneymakers I mean
it snowed like James Brown
I mean we kicked enough
zeroes loose the wind blew
our rental house down I mean
we danced hard I mean Sly

Stone and old systems fell
from the ceiling and we got
up-pa we got on up
in the dream

Body and Water

— for Bayo Olayinka Ojikutu

There's a body
under the floor,
twisted like tree
root, long gnarl
reaching like
memory, scratch
ing like history
at the planks
under our feet.
We like to say
we have no ears
for it. We invent
earbuds and expiration
dates. Tick tock.

The window's open,
the river's running
to fields, and water's
lapping at the porch,
history,
history,
history.
You can hear
the bodies
sloshing, sloshing.
You don't need
to binge-watch

forensics
to know skin
means something.
It's not that hard
to read a story.

Knock knock.
Who's there?
Nobody.
Nobody who?
Nobody
with a name
or a dental record
or a toe tag
because topical's
temporal, because
bodies are political
when they mean
something specific
to someone.
Write that down.

The river outside
your window,
seeping under
the door,
is perfumed
with bodies, bloated
flowers, pink sponges
turning by chains

and concrete blocks
under covered bridges
called Sands of Time,
called Sunday Drive,
called White Wash,
called TV Forensics,
called Kiss My Ass.

Leave the casket
open and it's a poem
and the poem
will say there's a toll
water must pay
to remain water
and the water
will say the same
about the poem.

Third Arm of the Lord Which Is for Coffee

— for Rick Canning and Brady Harrison

Once I walked in snow at 3 AM
and asked the land large questions.

About beginnings. Endings. Gain
and loss. About silence, when

and where it falls. And if no one's
there to hear it, what then?

I asked the land
because I believe in it.

Name an animal species
that has three legs. Kangaroos

don't count. Amputees are not
a species. Pop quizzes

are good for your brain.
One Saturday in the family van

I lost words, became a sock
of consonants in the ER,

amputation of song on a gurney.
In a hall just short of the machine

that reads bleeds I grew a syllable
that became a word and a phrase,

then a sentence. Nurse said miracle.
Doctor said hospital. I said daughters.

I said wife. I said their names, first
and middle. I built a ladder.

Some people seek limb removal
because they don't feel whole otherwise.

Addition by subtraction. The majority
of these travelers are middle-aged

white men. See body integrity
identity disorder. See self-amputation.

We are all travelers. Now is a good time
to leave, to go for a walk or coffee, ask

large questions, write your own poem.
I don't believe in the Lord,

but sometimes I have this dream
of addition, that I am the Lord,

that you believe me to have four limbs
like you, two arms, two legs,

your amputatable selves
made in my image. In my dream,

the one I'm having right now,
silence falls like sound in a forest

and it doesn't need you to hear it
and I no longer go on 3 AM walks

or carry pen and paper from room
to room in case the walls collapse

around me and I lose the ones
I love. My wife. My daughters.

Their names, first and middle.
Like animal amputees, some folks

lose limbs to cancer. I read a story
about a young man whose hand

was caught in a bear trap
and he sawed it off to save

his life. He knew how to do that.
If you don't, instructions are available

on-line. You'll need good reception
and a good knife. And a tourniquet.

Luck is also good. And nerve.
In this dream I'm having, I never lose

those names and I grow a third arm
for coffee or the odd poem. I grow it

not because I can but because
you can't. Because I'm the Lord.

Love's The Boy

Love's the boy stood on the burning deck
trying to recite "The boy stood on
the burning deck."
—Elizabeth Bishop, "Casabianca"

Thank you for the pirates, their skin
brag and rum, the leeches, the lashes.
and the long plank, wrists bound.
Especially that. I love the tipping
point, my feet bending wood
to water. Thanks for the burning
deck and the tilt of the ship
as it's going down. I like that
even more than the billowy sails
and the crow's nest. Love's the boy
kept his eyes open in the flames
and the water.

Thank you for the third floor
room, the curtain in the open
window, the coffee maker,
the neon and the drizzle,
the long hours of waiting
for the old poet to step out
of the limousine, the rifle
with scope and silencer.
I like his hat, the way it tilts

like talking. Love's the boy
loaded sonnets like cartridges
and fired them.

Thank you for the language
you took, and the ER,
thanks, and the dye docs shot
through me, groin to heart
to brain, thanks for the hot
and cold colors. Thank you
for the fences that shape fields.
Thank you for the language
you gave back, my daughters,
their names. Love's the boy
whiskied, stuttering, tossed.
And love's the boy returned
like dice, finite.

Dear No. 2 Pencil, Decomposing in Whiskey

At the end of the world,
a Tuesday, I crouched
with a blue notebook
in a concrete bunker
and drank schnapps
until my liver candied
like perfumed gristle
and I groaned
writing poems
is hard.

At my birth, a Sunday,
my mother, a nurse,
told me the story
about the woman
who stank. She lived
in a tower, that woman.
Or what might've been
a tower if the woman
had been a princess
and the tower
hadn't been
a mental ward.

Here on the deck
of this ship
that's tossing
in this bottle

my father cast
on roiling waters
under a picture-book   .
starry sky, I think
about that woman
and all the things
I should have told
my daughters
when I was alive
and smelled better.

Sometimes I get angry
and the bats
in my head win
and I enjoy
letting them go.
Worse than leaning
against the rough bark
of a tree and watching
your heart flap flap
flap off a cliff,
I would tell
my daughters,
is taking it back
when it returns.
Forgiveness, yes,
but forget nothing.
I didn't smell
all that good
when I was alive

and I am sorry
about the bats.

Some weeks I drop
a pencil in whiskey
to measure what's left
of my brain past stroke,
past dipthongs that stretch
for days like sound
might make sense of things.
I should have apologized
to my wife at my wake
for the long nights
of walking downstairs
to the kitchen and drinking
one double after another
and eating cold pork chops
in the open fridge door
when neighbors thought
the light meant I was writing
a poem. I should have said
poems are hard to write
after a second shower
when you still smell
like the dead sparrow
they found when they put
that woman in the tub
and spread her legs.

Decades before I died,
I pissed on my hands
so I could grip a bat
without gloves
and lace doubles
down both lines
and some nights
hit the ball out
of the park, twice.
Life was easier then.
Writing poems,
I'll tell my daughters,
is hard when all we do
is die and folks spend
money to make sure
no one smells us.
My daughters
play volleyball
and soccer,
run cross country.
It's not the same
and it probably is.

Three inches of water,
my mother, the R.N.,
told me, is what
they put in the tub
for that woman's
sponge bath.
Mental wards,

she had to know,
help a story,
make us look
at the wrong thing.
No one thought
to look there,
inside her.
I'm guessing
the story
has holes.
So do we.
We are nothing
without them.

Soundtrack for Last Words

Whiskey cleans the whiskey glass.

"St. Thomas," the first of five tracks on Sonny Rollins' *Saxophone Colossus*, references the Virgin Islands, his parents' homeland.

The ceilings of each of the three bedrooms in our flat-roofed house were succulent by design.

Each night, when they were young, I walked the perimeter, pushed at the damp ceilings when it was raining, and checked our sleeping daughters for breath or movement.

"St. Thomas" borrows the tune of the folk song "The Lincolnshire Poacher."

Some nights, as I typed, the pocket of branches just outside the window was still as ink in a cup.

Some nights I cleaned the whiskey glass more than once.

Late one summer evening, that window open, I listened to *Saxophone Colossus* for the first time.

"You Don't Know What Love Is" was written for an Abbott and Costello movie.

If you want to clean a mirror, vodka's better than whiskey.

I remember A is for aphasia, B is for bad brain or bruise songs screwed tight in a jar of bothers, and C is for cowboy who saved the day with a joke about the horse he rode in on.

I hope I would poach what we need if it comes to that.

Sleeping daughters and their sleeping mother my woman and my whiskey glass.

I walk, I check, I pour, I count.

I know what love is.

"Strode Rode," written by Mr. Rollins, is the last song on side one.

I want to say when the time comes "I took what we needed," but I think I took what I needed.

I add S is for stroke to the list of wounds.

Whiskey splashes over ice in the whisky glass I clean with whiskey.

I know sometimes foam rises against steep, littered banks.

I know stroke is the monster within.

For three weeks I listened to *Saxophone Colossus* once or twice an evening and wrote while I imagined the succulent ceilings were breathing with or against me.

"Moritat," the first of two songs on the second side, references "Mack the Knife," a monster improved by song.

Aphasia rose and fell like F for foam one afternoon.

My banks are steep and littered and wet.

I bruise song how I can.

There's a joke here about Whiskey River, the stroke I use to swim upstream.

Rhyme is everything in song.

X is for what done me wrong.

"Blue 7," an improvisational masterpiece, moved through three solos each night as I counted our four daughters, checked the ripe ceilings during rain, and wrote my last words.

I found the walls that made the hole.

Learned diamonds from coal.

Whiskey cleans the whiskey glass.

Moon Aubade

Last night I sang
the moon's a plate
of cheese and plums

Last night you sang
the moon's a song
to pluck and strum

And now it's light
And now the sun
says time to leave
We sing the moon
And now the sun
says time to leave

Last night I sang
the moon's a shield
to block the dawn

Last night you sang
the moon's a sheet
to lie upon

And now it's light
And now the sun
says time to leave

We sing the moon
And now the sun
says time to leave

(Repeat)

Acknowledgments, Appreciations, and Attributions

Grateful acknowledgments go to the following venues for publishing many of the poems in this collection (often under other titles): *New Letters, Your Impossible Voice, The Tusculum Review, The McNeese Review, The Museum of Americana, Sleipnir,* and *Hobartpulp.*

***

I've never listed thanks before because it's easy to forget someone. So first, let's mow the field of appreciations in wide swaths of friends and family: Madison County, Champaign County, Macon County, SIUE, and University of Illinois. I raise a glass of home brew in your direction. Yes, you.

Next I yodel my long if too late thanks through the ether to Okla Elliott (1987-2017), force of nature whose first name I gave to the river of writer-friends he led me to, among them Sean Karns, Kyle Minor, David Bowen, Duff Brenna, Rikki Rycraft, Thomas E. Kennedy, Renee Ashley, Kathy Graber, Walter Cummins, and Martha Collins. Okla River, may you run forever. I should yodel the same for another force of nature, Eric Miles Williamson, and all the friendships his friendship brought me: Ron Cooper, Charlie Alcorn, Tom Williams, Joe Haske, Alex Thiltges, Jean-Luc Bertini, Pete Fairchild, John Dunn Smith, Patrick

Michael Finn, William Hastings, and the ubiquitous others. Though Big E opened the tab, I should pay it.

After *Uncontainable Noise*, I said I was moving on to fiction. Then childhood friend Lois Byers and poet-designer-editor-publisher Susan Yount, in their different ways, made *Overpass* both necessary and possible. So I said it again. Later, poetry, main squeeze. And meant it until Karen Biscopink Farmer emailed to ask me if I had any poems for the inaugural issue of *Your Impossible Voice*. I lied, said yes, wrote a couple at the deadline, and here I am for another round. Heroes of mine, those three.

To others of you who promoted or translated or taught or improved my poems, invited me to visit, to contribute, to do an interview, I owe far more than this poor downpayment of inky thanks, folks like Tyehimba Jess, Tim Parrish, Xiaorong Jajah Wu, Larry Hanley, Kathleen Kirk, Clare MacQueen, Mairin Allen, Geri Doran, Chad Simpson, Jim Sullivan, Robert Grindy, Rosemarie King-Grindy, Jim Hicks, Michael Thurston, Emily Wojcik, Lee Furey, Clay Matthews, Octavio Quintanilla, Aënne Troester, Jeff Hendricks, Gianmarc Manzione, Sarah Meltzer, Sara Wainscott, Al DeGenova, Nina Corwin, Lea Graham at *Atticus Review*, Andrew McFadyen-Ketchum at *poemoftheweek.com*, and John King at *The Drunken Odyssey: A Podcast about the Writing Life*.

Upstate brothers Garin Cycholl and Bayo Olayinka Ojikutu, I owe you long pours of the best for the consistency of word and deed you've delivered over the years. John Griswold, downstate brother, the accountants have hired detectives who will find you. Time for you to pay your tab. David Wright, brother who pays his lunch and bar debts up front, the real debt is mine. Diguedos. Mark Sanders, out-of-state brother, I owe you beers on the back porch for your belief. Brady Harrison and Rick Canning, my Buffalo Jump Brothers, there from the start, ain't no river deep enough to hold all I owe you two.

And Lillian Bertram, Davendaughter if you weren't my elder in many ways, how to put a value on the years, the example of your discipline and invention, the shared confidences, the co-poeming? You tell me.

The rest of you? Return to the wide swaths in the second paragraph. I put you there with my mother, my sisters, and my life, Lynn. Excellent company.

Now the sun/ says time to leave.

I mean it this time.

(Repeat.)

***

"Dear Horse I Rode In On" includes a sentence I overheard John Dudek say in a teachers' conversation about the overuse of rhyme in introductory poetry workshops: "Rhyme is everything in song." The sentence repeats later in "Soundtrack for Last Words."

"In the Dream of Rhyming Nicki Minaj" samples "whiplash" and "blink fast" from Ms. Minaj's contribution to the posse cut of Kanye West's song "Monster."

"End of the Line" is a radical rewrite of Tomas Tranströmer's eleven-line poem "Tracks," which opens "2am: moonlight. The train has stopped" and closes "2am: bright moonlight, few stars."

"Night of Zeroes on the Loose" borrows the phrase "zeroes on the loose" from Wislawa Szymborska's "Possibilities."

"Body and Water," following Philip Levine's treatment of race in America, borrows the location "Kiss My Ass" from his magnificent "They Feed They Lion."

"Soundtrack for Last Words" samples my own lyrics from "Once I Had a Sorrow," a song I wrote with Bruce "Bruiser" Rummenie for our CD *This Noise in My Blood* as well as "Dear Horse I Rode in On," the first poem in this collection. Sonny Rollins' studio album *Saxophone Colossus* was released by Prestige Records in 1956.

CPSIA information can be obtained
at www.ICGtesting.com
Printed in the USA
FSHW012101140220